THE AMAZING
Mrs T.

A Whimsical but True Tale,
by Mrs Thrush

Translated by Tony Spite

To order additional copies of this book, contact:
Xlibris
0800-443-678
www.xlibris.co.nz
Orders@ Xlibris.co.nz

ISBN: Softcover   978-1-5434-9630-7
        Hardcover   978-1-5434-9631-4
        EBook   978-1-5434-9629-1

Print information available on the last page

Rev. date: 04/28/2020

There is an old Chinese proverb:

'If you save a life, you are responsible for that life.'

THE AMAZING MRS T.

This is where it all began – and nearly ended. In Mr S's lilypond in his lovely garden in Paraparaumu, a beachside town in New Zealand.

It was Spring in 2018 and I was a fat and fluffy little thrush, only a few weeks old, and my mother had just taught me to fly.

Mum had always told me to enjoy Mr S's garden, after all we were born near the top of the fence with the neighbours, and, because there were lots of cats in the area, our nest was cleverly hidden away in a tangled thicket of Jasmine and Bignonia. So I had to learn to fly very quickly when I was eventually shoved out of our nest by Mum and Dad.

She said there were lots of snails, slugs and worms to be found in the garden, but told me never to go near the pond. Of course, I was adventurous and having just discovered the joy of flight, I thought I knew everything.

I thought I could hop quite happily on to a water-lily leaf and splash about in the water, but before I knew it, I was under the water – mainly because a great big vulgar blackbird with a huge yellow beak had flopped into the pond and was thrashing around having a swim and washing himself. It gave me such a fright, I fell off the lily leaf. And now I was sinking with all my baby feathers getting waterlogged. Nobody had taught me how to swim and I was drowning!

Luckily for me, Mr S. was gardening nearby at the time and heard all the frantic splashing going on. He shooed the blackbird away and carefully pulled me out of the water and laid me down in the sun on the warm path nearby. I lay there wet, exhausted and petrified. Mr S. continued his gardening, but came over every so often to turn me over and check on me. Slowly I recovered.

Once I had dried out, my first thought was to get back to the safety of the fence, so I hopped gingerly off into the garden's undergrowth out of sight and eventually made it back to the nest.

Mr S. didn't see me go, and couldn't find me in the garden, so for a long time wondered if I had survived and was alright. I think he really worried about me.

Three or four months later I had matured quite a bit and was flying around enjoying myself one sunny morning when I found myself in his garden again. I realised that I hadn't really thanked him properly and, as his door was open, I hopped boldly in to where Mr and Mrs S. were having their breakfast. I came up beside his chair and fixed him with what I thought was a 'beady' eye and hoped he would recognise me.

Surprisingly he did. He at once said to Mrs S. "Look who's turned up at last – it's Miss Thrush – the one I saved from drowning in the pond!" (I don't know how he knew I was a 'Miss' Thrush because my brother and I look exactly the same! I suppose it was a lucky guess.) They immediately gave me some delicious bits of grained bread and some of their weet-bix and a few bits of apple. I was in seventh heaven. Apparently, I was the only bird that had ever walked into their house, and that's how they knew it must have been me.

And so all through that summer, from December to April, I hopped in and visited them for breakfast and often lunch as well.

However, much to their puzzlement, and concern, I then vanished again until November 2019.

I was of course extremely busy – building nests and having broods of my own, having become MRS Thrush with the partner I had found. We thrushes are much more industrious than blackbirds and have at least three broods a year, so we have to spend a lot of time building and rebuilding nests (sometimes if we get desperate we even use an old blackbird's nest, and they get very cross if we do. But they are typical bullies so that if two of us thrushes confront them, they take off squawking angrily!)

And then there is the laying of the eggs, the endless sitting on them, through all weathers, and the eventual hatching of the brood. And then the constant feeding of them - sometimes up to three, four or even five hungry little mouths! Luckily Mr Thrush helps me all the time – apart from the laying of course!

Painting by Mrs S.

So it wasn't until the early summer of 2019 that I was ready to return to visit Mr and Mrs S. and get to know them even better and, of course to catch up on a decent food supply.

And what a surprise they got! Because not only were they pleased to see me again, they realised eventually that I had brought two of my latest brood with me and they could see what I had been doing all winter.

We landed, or in the sake of the children, crash-landed, on the lawn near where Mr S. was busy gardening around the pond. So to calm down my babies, who were very flustered by then, not only because of their rough landings but also because I was introducing them to this huge man.

So we quickly flew up on to his garden seat.

Mr S. looked up from his gardening that day and there we were, sitting on his garden seat, me and two rather plump children! Or fledglings, as they are called. I don't think he realised they were mine until he caught me feeding one of them in the sitting room later.

I felt much more familiar and relaxed in the house now and though I could continue feeding in the kitchen, and showing the youngsters where they could get a good feed, I could also roam around the house and fly up onto the chairs and sofas.

I even explored into the bedrooms and sat on Mr S's bed! He only found out that I had been there because I left a small contribution! Unfortunately, the children soon thought they could have the run of the house too, and Mrs S. got very cross when they started leaving contributions on all the sofas, chairs, cushions, carpets and rugs. I think it is going to be a relief to them when we leave.

On one occasion I decided to settle down on a chair for a bit of a rest. That amused Mr S. "Bumptious Mrs T. !" he said. And that's about when he started calling me the Amazing Mrs T.

I could build a nest here!

Might have a read of that mag.

Oops! Caught feeding a baby inside.

The fledglings feeding in the kitchen.

Sometimes Mr and Mrs S. slept in, so I had to wait patiently at the door. Very annoying!

After a while, my children grew so fat and bossy that they were competing with me for the food that I had so carefully taught them where to find. They grew bigger than me and started chasing me away. They were very rude. One of them had even taken over my nest to start her own brood, so I will have to start building another one this year. Damned cheek!

However, Mr and Mrs S's house was still mine, so I learnt how to range around the chairs and sofas to keep out of the children's way when they were about.

I landed here and was only 40 centimetres from Mr S. when he took this photo. I think he thought I was going to swoop onto his weet-bix!

Good view of the garden from here.

I will miss all this when autumn comes.

Oh dear. One of the children – NOT me! Don't tell Mrs S.

Sometimes we are left to wait outside with the sparrows, which is quite rude!

One morning I flew into the house at breakfast-time, extremely agitated and warning Mr S. that I was in danger. He wondered why I was fluttering my tail feathers, prrping loudly and was looking so flustered, when he suddenly noticed a great big ugly tabby cat at the door and saw what the fuss was all about. The cat was stalking me!

Mr S. wasn't quite fast enough to take a photo, but this is what it looked like!

As quick as lightning, Mr S. reached for the nearest thing in front of him and flung the Marmite jar at the cat and shouted, and it fled, over the fence and away. (Luckily for me, Mr S. always has Marmite on his toast with his boiled egg.)

Phew! prrp, that was a close shave.

I stayed in the house and followed Mr S. around for the whole morning after that nasty fright, until I thought the coast was clear and I could fly home.

I really like it when Mr S. is gardening, I follow him around for hours and he chatters away to me, and his neighbours think he is potty, but he doesn't seem to mind. I understand everything he says but I don't think he understands when I say "Prrp" back. And I do a lot of "Prrping"!

We were working in the vegetable garden the other day, picking some silver beet for their dinner and also some rhubarb for Mrs S. to stew up for their pudding, when I let out a huge "PRRP" and jumped on a large snail which I took over to the path and thumped it on its shell until it broke and I could eat the snail inside. It was succulent and delicious! Mr S. let me do it and sighed "Nature is cruel sometimes." I replied "Prrp. Yeah. What about cats and us?! – and your lettuces."

Me, amongst the silver beet and rhubarb.

Good hunting this day – another snail!

It's fun too, when Mr S. empties the compost bin. The worms were fantastic!

Watching and waiting. Worms galore!

This year has been a long, hot and dry summer, so we birds have needed extra food and lots of water. We do NOT drink from the dangerous pond of course, but luckily Mr S. has kept our water bowls full all the time. Unfortunately, one of them is right under a ledge where Mrs S. feeds the wretched sparrows and they poop everywhere, so he has to be cleaning it out all the time.

"Just as bad as Mrs Thrush and her wretched children pooping all over the carpet inside!" says Mrs S.

My favourite drinking bowl, in the saucer under the pot!

I always fly in for lunch with Mr and Mrs S. They usually have it out in the sun under their archgola.

They often have croissants, which I love, and is a change from the rye or grain bread, but this day I flew in and it was a very odd meal!

They called it "Tomatoes on prosciutto on dark rye." YUK! I think they imagined they were on the Italian Riviera! Luckily Mr S. saw the problem and went off and got me some croissants. They were a bit stale and he apologised to me because he knows I prefer them fresh and warm.

Bliss! Give me a croissant, any day. I'm really getting quite sophisticated.

So here we are in March again, the start of autumn, and soon I will have to fly off and disappear again. I will find my usual partner and start preparing a nest and going through all the rigmarole of having a few more broods. Makes me feel quite old just thinking about it!

Thought I would have a last look around Mrs S's kitchen though. There are always a few crumbs to snap up. Look at all the lemon marmalade Mrs S. has made!

And one last sunbathe under the archgola:

And then I'll be off! "Prrp"

And so to this year's brood…………..

Five fledglings are going to keep me and Mr Thrush very busy!

THE AUTHOR.

Tony Spite.

After writing an extensive history of his family and ancestors over a long period of years, and editing his wife's own family history, Tony Spite felt the urge to keep on writing, but did not know where to start.

When Mrs Thrush fell unexpectedly into his life about two years ago, he realised there was an intriguing little story he could write for his eleven grandchildren. At first he wrote it from his point of view, but soon decided that to tell the story from Mrs Thrush's bird's eye view would be more fun.

And so 'The Amazing Mrs T.' was created.

Where Tony had not taken photographs of various scenes, his wife Jenny painted the pictures.

Printed in the United States
By Bookmasters